Stories from the
Arroyos

Stories from the Arroyos

Kathy Carpenter

Stories from the Arroyos

Copyright © 2019 by Kathy Carpenter. All rights reserved.

No part of this publication may be reproduced, stored in a retrieval system or transmitted in any way by any means, electronic, mechanical, photocopy, recording or otherwise without the prior permission of the author except as provided by USA copyright law.

The opinions expressed by the author are not necessarily those of URLink Print and Media.

1603 Capitol Ave., Suite 310 Cheyenne, Wyoming USA 82001
1-888-980-6523 | admin@urlinkpublishing.com

URLink Print and Media is committed to excellence in the publishing industry.

Book design copyright © 2019 by URLink Print and Media. All rights reserved.

ISBN 978-1-64367-700-2 (Paperback)
ISBN 978-1-64367-699-9 (Digital)
09.08.19

CONTENTS

Acknowledgments 7
Introduction..9
Our New Home In America..11
The Company Store 18
Smithy 22
Fun And Games 26
So Many Friends!..29
Mason Jars 33
My Collections..36
Carnation Milk 40
Cooking And Baking...43
The Mine Disaster 47
Grandmother's Gift 51
My Assignment 55
The Family Secret..58
The Wailing Wall 62
La Familia 65
No Privacy 69
A Difficult Decision 72
The Haunted House 76
A Sad Story 79
The Slingshots...82
The Mine Closing..85
Stories From The Arroyos...89
About The Author..91

ACKNOWLEDGMENTS

I wish to thank my dear friend Sue Ellen Hogan for her honest opinion regarding my stories. As she corrected my writing errors, she also encouraged me to get my manuscript published.

Another friend I wish to thank is Suellen Levy. By sharing her many years working with children, she helped me to focus my ideas and refine my stories.

To all those people who were surprised that I could write anything, I thank you for not discouraging me. I enjoyed the looks of surprise on your faces as I explained what I was writing. Not one of you said that it was a crazy idea.

Most important, I wish to thank my elementary school teachers. They performed miracles by teaching classes of more than fifty students in one classroom to read and write. Their patience and perseverance, plus positive reinforcement, has been the model for my teaching career.

Finally, thank you to all my readers who take time to enjoy the stories.

INTRODUCTION

Your first question might be, "What is an arroyo?" An arroyo is a water-carved gully in a very dry area, like a desert. When the mountain snows and the ground snows melt, the waters run downhill to a creek or river. With this runoff, anything that is on the ground is washed along. As you walk the fields in southern Colorado, you can see where the dirt is washed away from an area. Along with the dirt, anything lying on the ground is washed into the runoff, the arroyo. Over the years in southern Colorado, these runoffs have carried with them pieces of the history of the coalmining era.

The coal-mining days are over in this part of Colorado. Red piles of slag rock dot the landscape at the old mine sites. Crumbling foundations can be seen along the roads. Old sites can be found tucked among the groves of piñon and juniper, each place scattered with broken pottery, shards of blue and white glass, strips of stiff, weathered leather and rusted tins. Arroyos have collected debris as it was washed down from these places, carrying memories of the coal camp times to a final resting place, and burying these pieces of history beneath the adobe clay dirt common in this high desert area.

No one knows the exact source of the treasures or junk, as some people might view these, which are found as one walks the arroyos. But these items were at one time important to the people in the mining camps. They were a vital part of life for families living, laughing, and struggling in the coal camps. Life was hard and money was scarce, but everyone helped one another. By overcoming the obstacles of language, cultural differences, religion, and economic status, these miners and their families were strong in character and filled with hope and dreams.

As I walked through the arroyos and abandoned coal camps, I photographed some of these broken, rusted, frozen-in-time pieces of history and spent time thinking about how they might have been used, what the people were like, and what their life was like. These stories grew out of how I imagined these articles might have been used.

STORIES FROM THE ARROYOS is a book of historical fiction stories which come from the coal-mining era in southern Colorado during the early years of the twentieth century. The stories here are written from the viewpoint of children around ages nine to thirteen. They are told to remind us of days lost in history, and they can still influence us today. I invite you to read these stories through the eyes of a young child. When you read these stories, my hope is that you will hear the laughter, feel the losses, and see the activity in the camps.

It is with gratitude that we reflect on these people and celebrate their legacy of dreams passed on for us to enjoy. Enjoy your trip back in time to when life was different, yet maybe not so very different at all.

—Kathryn Carpenter

Stories from the Arroyos

OUR NEW HOME IN AMERICA

Papa and Mama are the bravest people I know. We came from Russia. In the Russian language, I call them Nana and Mum. If I use the proper words of father and mother, they are "OTEU I MATb," which sounds like "Maht and Otets."

Because you might have trouble remembering these words, I will just call them Papa and Mama.

Why did we come to America? Well, Russia is a beautiful country but there is what Papa calls a "revolution" going on. The people are killed by soldiers. Russia is always at war, and the country is being taken over by other countries. That's just the way it has always been. Our friends died, the village was burned, and we were all scared. Papa learned about the "American Dream" from letters he received from friends in America. He knew that if his family was to survive, he had to take them to America. The American Dream was that of having a happy life, making money, having a peaceful place to live, and going to good schools.

Otets, I mean Papa, said we had to leave because of the revolution. He explained it to me like this: "Svetlana, the Russian Revolution is political and social unrest. It is terrible! People have been forced to move out of their homes. Soldiers are living with families against their will. Crops are stolen from the farmers to feed the soldiers. In some places, the crops are just burned to the ground. We wanted a better life rather than all this arguing and fighting. We left Russia to find a better place where we could be happy and free."

In Russia, we lived near the coastline. I loved the water and the changing clouds. The wind blew every day. My friends and I went to the coastline often, and I always had sand in my clothes and shoes. The grass was richly green because of all the moisture. The trees almost reached the clouds. I loved the ocean and the beach. I climbed the trees with my friends, and we played lookout for ships passing by, wondering where they were coming from and where they were going. We made up stories about their journeys. I miss all of this beautiful land.

We left Russia in May 1899 and arrived in New York City three months later. I remember smelling the ocean air every day and all day. I thought about the homeland we were leaving and missed it already. The ocean was delightful to look at when we first started out, but after a few weeks, everyone just wanted to get safely to America.

Many of the people on the ship could speak Russian. I listened as the women talked about their homes and what they could not bring along on the trip. All of us had to leave many things behind. Our favorite chairs, our books, kitchen wares, and sewing machines were all back there. It was terribly sad listening to them as they talked about what they left back in Russia. Many of the women were trying to hide their tears while they spoke as if leaving their beloved possessions was not anything hard.

They talked about cooking and baking. They wondered if they could prepare the same foods in America. They wondered if, in America, the government would ration flour, just as they did in Russia. Some women read letters from relatives in America that described the houses, the clothes, and the stores. They read that there were so many different stores and all of them had many different things inside. In Russia, a store had only a few kinds of things, likes shoes or coats. In American stores, there were hundreds of different shoes and coats. How do they do this? I tried to imagine what that would look like, but my mind got all jumbled and tired trying to think about these things.

The men would talk about agriculture, fishing, and building. I listened to their conversations and their laughter for hours. They wondered what kind of fish lived in the rivers and lakes. They wondered about the kind of trees that grew there and if the lumber would be suitable for building homes and furniture. They had heard stories of pioneers in America who, years ago, traveled in wagons and made homes out of dirt. They laughed at this, and most of them just could not understand how the "soddies" (the people who built sod houses) could live like that.

The men would always end their day of talk by saying something like, "We will be free to live the way we want. Our sons will not be forced to into the army. We will be happy families instead of living in fear. Our children will go to schools and learn to be great men." The men talked about determination. I asked him what that meant. He sat back and replied, "Determination means that you will do everything possible to get what you want. Remember this, my dear Svetlana: you will get nowhere in life without determination. You make life what it is."

Sometimes the ship would get caught in a storm. We rocked and rocked because of the huge waves. People got sick from all the motion. Even Mama got sick for a while. This made Papa feel guilty because he was the one who talked her into leaving Russia. No one on the ship knew what the travel would be like or what to expect. We just knew we had to get out of Russia before the war destroyed our homes and us.

When we arrived in America three months later, we were processed to make sure we had legal papers and no diseases. There were hundreds and hundreds of other people from all over the world. They all looked as poor as us. I talked to some other girls my age who could speak Russian. They too were terribly frightened of what was going to happen. They were also wondering where we would live, what school would be like, and if we would always see fighting and killing like in Russia.

We were called immigrants at the processing center. It was here that we found out people were going to different places in America because many had relatives who had arrived months earlier and found work. We had friends in New York, but we were not staying there. Papa said we will go west, where he will work at farming. This is what he knows best.

Our land trip across America took us many weeks. We traveled by train and wagon. We were tired and hungry. By now it was too late to turn back, but we were too tired to go on. Papa said, "We are survivors. We will make it!" He said, "Life will always have hard times. You must learn to work with what you have and always have a dream of something better." He said that if we go back to Russia, we will have no home, no land, no money, and the soldiers would probably kill us. That was reason enough for me to keep on going in America.

When we finally arrived in southern Colorado, other people from our homeland were already there. They invited us to stay with them. You can't imagine how delightful it felt to sleep in a bed, even though it was with four other people. Some children led us to a little river, where we had a decent wash. It was the first cleaning since we left Russia many months ago.

Papa set about looking for work. No farmers or ranchers were being hired, but he got a job at one of the mines. He doesn't know anything about mining. The boss said he is strong and smart and will learn quickly. Since other Russians are working there, he figured he could learn right along with them. At least he can talk to them in the same language.

I am enrolled in a school that is owned by the mine. We all will learn to speak English. We are told that when in school, we cannot speak our native language and that everything we say must be in English. In the first few weeks, the school room was exceptionally quiet. The only voice we heard was the teacher's. Slowly we picked up words from her and repeated them until we were all saying some English words. I was as surprised as everyone because English is hard. We are all from different countries. I would guess there are fifteen different languages in that class of twenty-five children. We all anticipate the day when the teacher gives us praise for our attempts at English.

One thing I like about our new home in America is that we can talk to anyone, anywhere, anytime. There aren't any soldiers who walk around and give us orders about what to do and not to do. I like this freedom. I also like going to school in America because we can laugh and have fun while we are learning. I don't remember ever laughing in school when I was in the old county. Someone did laugh once, and he got a beating. In the Russian school, we could not run outside when the school bell rang at the end of the day. We had to march out, single file, standing straight and looking forward. In America, we can run, laugh, tease, and help one another whenever we want.

Papa and Mama are glad we are learning to speak and read English because then we can get suitable jobs when we are older. In the evenings, all of us children teach our parents the words we learned. They think words are hard to learn. It takes them longer. One thing I have noticed is that even though we learn the same words, everyone says the words differently. I asked my teacher why this is and she says people from different countries have what we call accents. I like the different accents. Mama says it makes a colorful language. I don't know about colorful, but it sure makes the language interesting.

I miss Russia. The land in America is extremely dry. There is no green grass, no oceans, and no fresh air coming off the oceans. The trees are smaller. If you go up a hill or a ridge, you can see for miles, but you don't see the ocean. The only thing that is the same is the wind. When I close my eyes on a windy day, I can picture in my mind the ocean and the birds, the waves and the large fish. My heart gets sad because I miss the old country.

Around here, there are mountains and runoffs called arroyos. They fill up when the snow melts and when we get thunderstorms, which is not often. There are also cacti. These are new to me. I tried picking a cactus flower once, and oh, did it pick me! The barbs are pointed and remarkably sharp. I guess this is so animals don't eat them; I don't know for sure. In school, we learned about the many kinds of cacti in this area. The teacher said the Indians used the yucca cactus roots to make soap. For my part, I will just keep a distance between me and any cactus!

    Papa goes into the mine every day. He said at first he was scared because it is small and dark. He often can't stand up straight because of the low ceilings. He has tools that he carries and a helmet that has a light on it. Mama packs a lunch pail and lots of drinking water for him. Some of the Russian workers put vodka in their pails instead of water. Papa says vodka gives him headaches and reminds him of unhappy times in Russia.

    Papa told us that the miners go hundreds of feet underground. Many accidents occur in the mines. There are explosions from gases, fires, flooding, and sickening air. Everyone comes out coughing from breathing the black coal dust. He is working twelve hours a day, six days a week. Papa's face, hands, and clothes are all black. Mama spends hours trying to clean his work clothes. No matter how hard she tries, the clothes never get clean!

    We have a nice house. It is just for our family. There are no soldiers here to force other people to live in our house. We have delicious food, and mother is a wonderful cook. We always have enough food for each person. No one ever has to give up his food for someone else. I sleep in a bed with only one other person. Papa says, "Just wait until you have more brothers and sisters! You'll have to share your bed with a lot more!" Then he always laughs, and mother always smiles.

    I have many new friends at school. We can do a many things without having to talk to one another. We play baseball, marbles, racing, and high- low rope games. I am learning to speak words in different languages by playing with people from the different countries. Mama says this is good but that no matter what, I cannot use any curse words. I'm not sure what these are, but I know that someday I will find out.

    In our new home in America, I have many of the same chores that I had back in Russia. The only difference is that we do not have cattle or sheep or chickens. Papa says someday maybe we can get more land and have animals again. He is always thinking ahead and planning and dreaming.

Anyway, my chores are to keep the yard clean of debris, like sticks, large stones, and things the wind blows in; water the flowers; and empty the night bucket. Papa is proud of our home and wants to let everyone know this by how well he keeps his house and yard.

It's getting late and I must end my story. When the wind is blowing outside, we are safe inside. Our home in America is a dream that has come true for Papa and Mama. I like it here too. Even though there are many differences in work, countryside, and houses, I am happy and we are free. Freedom is not something we will give up ever again.

Kathy Carpenter

THE COMPANY STORE

We are a family from Sweden. We all know how to work hard. Papa works extremely hard every day, except on Sunday. He has huge, strong arms from digging coal out of the rocks. He says coal mining is terribly hard work and that I should stay in school so I can have a better life than he has.

Papa says he gets paid about $5.24 a day, but that's not what he actually brings home. He uses a pick axe and shovel that belong to the company. He has to pay to have the pick axe sharpened. That money is taken from his pay. When any of us get sick and need to see a doctor, that cost is taken from his pay too. We can only use the company doctor that is in our camp.

The company also owns our house. We pay rent to stay here. The rent is based on the number of rooms we have. Some camps charge according to the number of light bulbs in the house. When any of us need clothes, we don't buy these from the company store. All the families that are our friends pass used clothes to other families. Sometimes the clothes need some sewing or patching. When all of your friends are wearing sewn or patched clothes, no one makes fun of anyone else. This is just the way it is.

I don't mind the used clothes, but the used shoes usually hurt my feet. One day a kid from the city came to the camp all dressed in new clothes and new shoes. She saw us in school and said to her mother, "They sure look poorly in their ragged clothes and shoes that don't even match!" I wonder what she meant. Our clothes aren't ragged. They are sewn and patched. I do not know what that girl meant by shoes not matching. City kids are surely different.

When the city girl walked back to her waiting buggy, she slipped on a patch of ice and landed on the ground near some melting ice and mud. What a sight it was! Oh well, now she kind of looked like the rest of us!

The only place we can buy groceries is at the company store. The money Papa earns is always paid in scrip. Scrip comes in varying amounts. Before he is paid, however, the company store takes out their share of scrip for groceries. I know how to add scrip, but I don't know how to count real money. I never even had real money in my hands.

Anyway, what I want to tell you is about my trips to the company store. I go every week with either my older sister or brother or just tag along when they go with Mama. The storekeeper doesn't speak Swedish, but we can still talk to him with signs and by pointing. Too bad we can't speak to each other because of the language barrier, but that is common in the mining camp. There are so many different languages here because people come from many different places. In my camp, there are people from Scotland, Ireland, Lithuania, Russia, Croatia, Germany, Latvia, Italy, and so many other places. We learned how to spell the names of these countries in school because this is where the other students are from. The teacher is remarkably smart to know how to spell all these names!

I got sidetracked on my story about the company store so I'd better get back to it. The store is in the "neighborhood," just like in the big city. One store carries supplies for anything we need. Well, I should say almost anything we need. If there is something Papa needs and he can't get it at the company store, he will barter or make a deal with someone in the camp. That means he will trade something for it or do some work for the person in exchange for what he needs. Papa says that's the way it was done in the old country.

On the shelves are hundreds and hundreds of cans. I tried counting them once, but I only know how to count to one hundred so I guessed at the rest. Anyway, there are a lot of cans. Some have pictures on them, others just have words. I sometimes wonder where the cans go when they are empty. I think they go to the camp dump. I also see old cans in barrels and in boxes tossed all around the camp.

Mama says the company store "carries" canned goods. I don't think she uses the right word because a building can't carry anything. It can't even move, and it doesn't have arms or wheels! But I am not going to tell her that it is the wrong word; oh no, that is something children can't do. We can never correct an adult. That's the law!

The company store has cans filled with milk, some powders, and some things I've never heard of. There are lots of boxes too. These always have pictures. I think they have pictures on them so everyone who cannot read them can see what is in there, most of the time anyway. One time I had to buy baking powder and brought home baking soda. I liked the picture better.

There are things we never need to buy, like fruits and vegetables. Almost everyone has a small garden. People from the town sometimes bring fruit that we can trade for. Sewing and baked goods are good trading. We just never have actual money to give them. Sometimes they will trade for some scrip too. Mostly, they like to trade for something they don't have.

Besides having cans and boxes, the store also has clothes and shoes, and some tools and toys. It has tools for fixing things if something should break. There is nothing fancy in the company store like the store in the city. It does not have jewelry, sewing machines, wagons, fancy girl stuff or fun boy toys. We have to make our own. I will tell you about that in another story.

As I am learning to read, I like to go to the store just to try to read the posters, signs, and labels on the cans. I am getting better at that. Every time I go, I can read more words. Papa says reading English is important if I want to make something of myself. I want to make Papa proud of me.

People from all over the camp hang around the store. They talk about the weather, tools, mining, bosses, mules and horses, getting rich, and families. It is fun listening to grown-ups talk because they laugh a lot, they tease each other, and sometimes they say things that I haven't heard before. I remember one day they were talking about the ladies in the brightly colored dresses who were in the saloon. The stories made all the men laugh and laugh. I didn't understand what they were laughing about. After a while, I left to go play with friends my own age.

Anyway, this is my story about the camp store. Many workers and families don't like the way they get paid and that they have to shop only at the company store. They say it is the mine owners' way of keeping the money in the camp for themselves. I don't understand this, but I guess no one else does either.

SMITHY

My primary job, when I am not in school, is to feed and care for the mules. My father said that since I am ten years old and a very strong boy, I can help with the work and earn money to help the family.

I started working for the mining company last year when school was out for the summer. Father says I must stay in school and not quit. He says I should learn all I can from books and teachers so I don't have to work underground like he does.

I am glad that I got the job I asked for because I really like animals. I am a trapper for the mine. I open and close the mine doors when the mule trains go in and come out. Father told me that someday maybe I could work as a mule-driver. That is a man who takes the teams into the mine and hauls the filled coal cars out of the mine. Someone told me that mule-drivers get paid as much as $2.95 for ten hours a day. We don't get real money, though. We get paid in company scrip, which can only be used at the company store. Still, I can help buy food and shoes and sometimes a little candy. My parents are proud of me for wanting to work and help the family. I am proud to help my family too, but also very proud I get to work with the mules.

Mules haul the carts filled with coal out of the mines. The loads are heavy, and sometimes the mules really have to pull hard. Sometimes they get cuts from the rocks they walk over. Sometimes their shoes come off and they get sore feet. I admire them for the hard work they do. Some miners don't realize it, but mules are actually more valuable than workers because they are harder to replace. They work day after day, sometimes complaining by being stubborn and not wanting to cooperate. But most of the time they just do their work.

I heard that if a miner hurts a mule, he gets fired. Mules are more valuable than people. The camp bosses pass the word to other camp bosses if a miner hurts a mule; then no one will hire him. That's how important the mule is!

Without mules, the coal cannot be hauled to the surface. Miners get paid by the ton. They must use picks and sledgehammers to break the rocks to get the coal out. Sometimes the miners must lie on the ground and use pick axes to dig the coal from the rocks. This is hard work, and the rock pieces and coal dust are always falling into their faces. They load the coal into carts that have wheels, and mules pull the load out of the mine.

Mules are hardworking animals, but they can also be stubborn. One day someone said to me that I was as stubborn as a mule. I thought he was saying something nice to me, so I said, "Thank you!" Everyone laughed. I didn't get the joke.

I am in charge of six mules. My favorite is one that I named Smithy. Smithy is also the name of the man who makes horseshoes and mule shoes. He is the blacksmith. I don't know why he is called a blacksmith because he is actually a white man. He has immense muscles on his arms. I bet he could bend an iron rod! He is from the country of Denmark but doesn't talk about his country very much. Maybe he misses his friends back there. He never talks about a family. So I guess I actually don't know much about him.

One day I told him that I named a mule after him and he smiled. His job is to make mule shoes. These are smaller than horseshoes and protect the mules' feet, or hooves, as they are actually called. Mules wear out their shoes very quickly because they are always walking on rocks.

Twice a day, I tend my mules. Sometimes I give Smithy grain and hay for his food, by hand. He seems to like the extra attention.

Sometimes Smithy, the mule, not the blacksmith, is so tired at the end of the day that he is too exhausted to eat. He also drinks a lot of water, which I have to carry from the river. Sometimes I think he will drink the whole river!

The part I like best about taking care of Smithy is rubbing him down and brushing him. He is brown and gray and has short hair. He has giant ears and a mighty big head. My father says that if I ever tell a lie that my ears will get big like Smithy's.

Time with Smithy the mule is my special time. Even though he is a mule, I still like to hug him. I get up close to his neck and smell his wonderful animal scent. My sisters think I am crazy for smelling my mule. Brushing him is so relaxing, for me and him. I hum when I brush him because Smithy likes the sounds I make. His eyes get droopy and he just relaxes. I guess this is kind of like a mother singing to her baby. Please don't tell my sisters that I hum to my mule. They will really tease me then.

I don't know what it is about animals that I like, but someday I want to take care of animals for a living. I think Smithy (the man, not the mule) said a person who does that a vet, and that is what I would like to be. I would learn to heal their wounds, stop their coughs, and even help when they have babies. I wonder if mules have babies. Yes, I would like to be a vet. I wonder if vets make money. I hope I get to go to school and learn about caring for animals. I watch Smithy the blacksmith hammer away on the anvil and know that it is extremely hard work. He builds muscles doing this, and he gets very sweaty. He says, "There is not better job for a man than working with his muscles." That might be true for some people, but I would like to do something to help the animals.

One day in school, the teacher asked us what we wanted to be when we grew up. Some of the kids said they never thought about it. Some said they wanted to be mothers with lots of babies, cooks for the camp, famous singers, and things like that. Some people want to be collectors. They walk the arroyos looking for treasures that they can sell or trade. Some people want to travel back to their homeland to see their friends. I said I wanted to be a vet. The teacher gave me a strange look and asked, "You want to be a vet, a veteran, a soldier?"

She wondered because I was from Eastern Europe and she knew about the problems and wars they had there.

I said, "No, a vet, a person who takes care of animals."

She said to me, "Oh, I see, you want to be a veterinarian!" Well, I had never heard that big word before, but it sounded like something important. She said, "That is very good, but you will have to study a lot." That is fine with me as long as I get to work with animals. I will do whatever I need to do to be a vet!

I must stop telling my story now. It is time to get supper for Smithy and the other mules. This is my job. I am responsible for their care. If I want to earn money for my family, I better get my work done, and after that comes the homework. Both are very important now!

FUN AND GAMES

One thing I learned early on is never to say, "I am bored. There is nothing to do!" You can think it, but don't say it! You can be sure a grown-up will find something for you to do very quickly!

As you know, there are lots of children in the coal camps because there are lots of families. Most of our time we are outside of school, we are playing games and having fun. Let me tell you about some of these games and you can see if you might want to play with us.

Everyone knows jump rope, hopscotch, and tag. There are many ways to play jump rope, hop scotch, and tag. We play horseshoes, all kinds of ball games, and many different card games.

Kids from the different countries all have their own way and their own rules. We try to learn as much as we can because the games are sometimes similar and we can win. Sometimes they are much harder, so we are challenged. Either way, we laugh a lot and have fun.

The younger kids from Germany like to play *Sadinens,* which in English is Sardines. It's an easy game. Someone is "it" and hides. Others search for "it," and when they find "it," they join "it." After a while, they are all crowded together like sardines in a can. The last person to find "it" and the others all crowded together is the loser and becomes "it" for the next game.

My friends from Mexico like to play *La Gallinita Ciega* (The Blind Hen). All you need is more than three people and a handkerchief. One person is the hen and puts the handkerchief over his or her eyes. Then he or she is turned around several times. Then everybody scatters, but not too far. The blind hen tries to find the others and guess who it is. If the guess is right, that person becomes the blind hen. We laugh a lot with this game because the blind hen actually looks funny reaching out, arms swinging, trying to find someone. He also bumps into a lot of things. Sometimes we laugh so much our sides ache!

Italian children play a game called *Lupo,* which means wolf. This game needs about seven players, and one person is the wolf. He faces one way, and the others line up some distance behind him. The group calls out to the wolf, "What time is it?" The wolf says a number and the line moves forward that many steps. They again ask the wolf, "What time is it?" Again the wolf calls out a number. Sometimes instead of saying a number, the wolf says, "I am hungry," and quickly turns around to tag as many players as he can before they make it safely back to the starting line.

All of us know how to play marbles, but the rules are different depending on where you are from. No one is an expert, so the games are all fair. We don't argue or fight if we lose. We just play another game. Eventually you find out what you are skilled at and stay with the group of kids playing that game.

No matter where the kids come from, they all know these games. I think this is surprising that people from all over the world know how to play the same games. There are different rules and such, but mostly the games are a lot alike.

Sometimes a group of three or four of us take a walk around the camp houses and look for things to use in making up games. Once I found a bent barrel hoop. I reshaped it to be round again and rolled it down a slope. I made up a game and taught it to others. I didn't name the game, but it goes something like this. You take turns rolling the hoop down a small slope. The person who rolls it the farthest and keeps it upright wins the game. You get a winner every time you play! The challenge comes when the slope is steep or rocky, and the hoop falls over after only a few feet.

My friend Andrae from France made up a game of toss the ball. We toss it into a hoop, and each time we throw it, we throw it differently. One time you have to throw it overhand, and then underhand, then over the shoulder, and so on. Each time you get it into the hoop, you get a point. The person with the most points wins. It's more fun when some girls play with us. They throw the ball all over the place!

On days when we can't be outside, like in the winter when it snows, we play board games, pick-up sticks, jacks, and easy games like that. These games aren't as much fun for us older kids.

I don't know why I like the fun and the games but I hope I never outgrow playing them. I learn other things besides just playing. When mother has me watch my brothers, we play a game they can do. When she wants me to sit with grandmother, we play checkers. I always enjoy spending time with my grandparents.

Mother says games are important to learn about cooperation and taking turns. She says playing fairly is important for when I grow up. She also says games teach me to share. No matter what I learn, I know I have fun and like to play.

Of course, you will never hear me say, "I'm bored," because there is so much to do! I just have to look around. Besides, I like to run and play and laugh a lot. Mother says all that energy is wasted on the young. She says they should save it because they will need it when they get old like her. She always makes us laugh.

SO MANY FRIENDS!

What is the best day of the week? *It's Saturday!*

Everyone gets together to play baseball on Saturdays. With over a thousand people in our camp, there are lots of teams for all the kids and the grown-ups. I play on the team with my friends from school. We call ourselves the Dynamites and no other team has ever beaten us.

After our chores are done in the morning, we gather in the back field and set up our diamond. We use flat rocks for the bases and bury the home plate rock in the ground. At first we didn't bury it. We got some wicked injuries when we would be at bat and hit the ball, only to trip and fall when we started running. I guess you could say we learned as we went along!

Usually we have real baseballs. These came from our dads and older brothers who got them after the adults were done with them. They were never actually very round because they were used so much. Sometimes the stitching was broken in places, but we didn't care. At least we had baseballs! One time the only hardball we had left was one with the cover torn off. The inside string was unraveling. Someone suggested we get some tar pitch and smear it on the ball. It sounded like a good idea, but we encountered a serious problem. When the pitcher tried to throw the ball, it wouldn't leave his hand! He tried holding on to it with just two fingers and then pitching it. If the batter did connect with the tar ball, it went *thud* and only flew a few feet and rolled in the dirt. The tar ball was a big mistake. The one who suggested the idea then got a new nickname. You guessed it: Tar Ball.

The bats were made of hard wood from the piñon and juniper trees. Someone would cut a piece of wood and then try to make it in the shape of a bat. Sometimes the bat would be too long or have bumps on it. That would make the ball go where no one was expecting. If the wood was rotten on the inside, the bat would crack and splinter into a million pieces. Fortunately we always had more bats. Broken bats were sometimes a danger for anyone watching!

We would use paint and draw a circle on the bat to make it look like the real thing. Sometimes the painted area looked pretty snazzy. One day a girl got a hold of her brother's bat and drew a figure of a doll in the circle. You should have heard the teasing from his teammates! He still used it, and he usually hit a home run. He was not embarrassed at all. They must have been a close family.

Someone almost always got hurt. Scrapes and cuts were part of the game. Usually someone's family member had some alcohol and a clean cloth to take care of the injuries. We never broke any bones, at least not on my team.

In the spring when we played, the wind would be blowing so hard that the adobe dust from the desert floor would get into our eyes and mouths. But the game would still go the full innings, or at least as long as the balls and bats held out. The wind is part of life here. People would look at you strangely if you ever said, "Oh good, another windy day!" No one likes it, but at least we don't have the terribly cold weather that we had in Finland, Poland, or Germany. Everyone agrees with that!

The heat in the summer is extremely dry and hot. Even when you sweat, it seems to dry right off your body. You get used to all the people smells when you are playing baseball. It is just part of the game. No one cares what you look like or how you smell as long as you can hit and catch the ball.

When it is downright hot, we have to take time-outs to get water and cool off. The water has a strange smell and an odd taste. The owner of the camp says that the smell and taste won't hurt us.

He says all the wells run with the mine wells and that we should be glad to have cool water. I don't know. My dad says the water in the mines gets very dirty. As it runs off, it flows past the mule sheds and the dump, and this really smells bad. Everything empties into the river. I think there are some not-so-good things about living in the mining camps.

We have two girls on our team. We are one of the few teams that have girls. Let me tell you why we have them. We have them because they are good players, as good as any of the other players! Sure the other teams tease us, but we stand up for them every time. Mother says someday those other boys will be older and want a date for the dance. She says to see how the boys behave then! Mother always knows what to say to make us laugh.

During our games, we all have two things that we have to be careful not to do: rip our clothes or ruin our shoes. We would be in for a scolding or worse when we got home. Some people don't wear shoes when they play. I think that would hurt their feet, but they say it doesn't hurt. They say it is the shoes that hurt their feet. I still haven't figured that out.

There are usually four or more games going on in our camp during the afternoon. The rules are not real strict and no one calls the plays. We just have fun. The adults play their games in another area. They have game rules. An umpire calls the plays. They need all this because sometimes the players make bets on who will win. Sometimes they drink and fight. Compared to them, our games are very tame.

After the afternoon games are won and lost, we sit around and talk about many things. I like this part best. We talk about our home countries, and I learn so much about places I know that I will never see. Some friends really miss what they had "back there" in their homeland, and others are happy to be here. We compare food and clothing and words. We tell stories. There are so many friends, and I learn something from all of them. We laugh and tease one another and no one ever gets mad.

I have lived here since we came from Finland, and even though school is difficult and work is hard, and the wind and heat are annoying, with great friends to play with and have fun with, this is a good place to be.

I am glad to be here. Saturdays will always be my favorite day!

MASON JARS

My name is Giuseppe and I came with my momma and papa from southern Italy. We had a small farm in the old county, but here in the Unites States of America, my papa is a miner and we live in a mining camp. Other people in the camp are also from Italy. We sing songs and do the dances we did in Italy. When we are together we speak Italian, but in school we must speak English. I hope I don't forget my Italian words!

The women talk about how hard life is here. They talk about the weather that it is too dry and windy to grow productive gardens. They say the only dependable thing here is that the clothes that are hung out on the clotheslines always dry very quickly. I agree that the sun does get very hot and the wind very bothersome.

I like to play with my friends and run up the hills and walk through the arroyos. We are always looking for things that might we worth something. So far we haven't found anything valuable that would make any money, so we are still poor. But we have fun anyway.

One rainy day, I was watching Mama put fruit into blue-colored jars. I asked her why the jars were blue. She said a man named Mason thought of making the jars blue so the light would not spoil the fruit. I asked why he didn't make them black instead of blue, and Mama just smiled and said, "Guiseppe, you have so many questions!"

A week later, a new family moved into the camp. I went to their house and peeked around the corner and heard someone call the man of the family "Mr. Mason." I ran home to tell Mama that a famous person moved into the camp. I just knew it had to be the same man who invented the Mason jar. I just knew it! Besides, how many other Mr. Masons are there in America?

One morning, I went to the company store for Mama. I saw Mr. Mason in the store. He was tall and dressed in clothes that were not usual for a miner. His clothes were unusually clean, and they didn't have patches all over like the otherminers. I wanted to talk to him but was afraid to because, after all, he was so famous, like the pope or Napoleon or President McKinley!

When he was busy looking at some axes, I moved closer to him and pretended to be looking at the tools too. He turned to me and said, "Hello, young man. Who might you be?"

I replied, "My name is Giuseppe." He reached out his hand and shook mine.

"Glad to meet you, Giuseppe. I am Mr. Mason. I just moved into the camp."

I smiled and said, "Glad to meet you too, sir."

I was so excited to have met such a famous person that I ran to tell my friends. They were impressed when I told them what happened at the company store. I told them that I would never wash that hand again because I touched a famous person. They all laughed.

When I got home, Mama was still canning and told me to get some more Mason jars from the shelf and wash them for her. *Oh no! What should I do? I cannot disobey mama, but if I wash the jars then the famous Mason touch will be washed from my hand!* I thought for a while, and then I carefully took the jars off the shelf and put them in the water to wash them. I asked Mama if she had a small jar that I could have. She gave me a small jar that once had jelly in it. I was so happy to have it! This would solve my problem! After I washed the jars for Mama, I carefully put some dishwater into my little jar and put the lid on it. I took the rest of the dishwater to the back door and threw it out into the yard like we always do.

My famous "Mason touch" was now safe in my jar! I hid the jar in my secret hiding place. Now I can keep this prize forever! To me, it is more valuable than gold! I can't tell anyone about the jar because someone might steal it. It's my prize. Only I know where it is!

MY COLLECTIONS

I am the richest fifth grader in our mining camp because I am a collector. I have boxes and piles of everything anyone could ever want. My friends nicknamed me Pack Rat. This is a mammal that lives in this area and collects everything: sticks, cactus, coins, jewelry, pencils, paper, food—you name it, a pack rat has it in his nest.

I don't mind the nickname because my friends just call me that because I collect everything and anything. You just never know when someone will ask, "Does anyone have a large bolt?" or "Does anyone have a wheel rim?" No matter what, my goal is to collect some of everything in the camp, no matter how small or large.

You may be wondering why I am interested in collecting things. My *pateras,* which means "father" in Greek, is a collector. When he lived in Greece, he lived in the countryside and worked in a vineyard. He made sure all the equipment and machinery were ready every day. He spent his evenings making repairs on the wagons, tightening loose bolts, and sharpening knives. He was highly skilled, and the owner of the vineyard liked my pateras, I mean my father. (It's hard to remember to use English words. I only use English in school. At home we always speak Greek.)

Pateras likes to talk about his life growing up in Greece. He talks about the big Olympic Game in Athens that he saw before he left Greece. He said the athletes were so strong and knew how to compete fairly. It was an exciting event, and people came from all over the world. Pateras tells stories about Greece in the evening when we have the family dinner. I wish I could see the beautiful countryside and many hills, all covered in green, and smell the Mediterranean Sea.

Pateras has always collected things. Mietra, my mother, said that is why she married him. Her father liked him because he was helpful in repairing anything that was broken. He always had the piece or part that was needed. She said, "Someday all that junk will come in handy and maybe make us rich!" We always laugh when she says this. We are not rich, just a poor miner's family living in Colorado.

One day at school, we were asked to bring something that we liked. We were supposed to go in front of the class, stand straight, talk about what we brought, and answer questions. We were practicing what the teacher called "public speaking." The night before that day, I was trying to decide what to take to school and what I could say about my stuff.

Going through my boxes, I found some nails, a metal bar, and some washers. Some pieces had rust on them, and my hands got dirty just holding them, but to me they were my treasures. Now I had to think about what to say about my treasures.

The next day at school, everyone was excited, and there was a lot of talk about what each person brought. There was clothes, bread, dishes, a baseball, a baby blanket, a new book, and paper and coin money from other countries. No one had the same thing that I brought and I was happy about that.

When it was time, each student walked to the front of the class, stood straight, and spoke about the thing she or he brought. Everyone had to speak their information in English. Now I was getting nervous!

The stories that were told were happy, sad, and funny. The boys looked so scared and their faces sometimes turned red as they spoke. You could tell that very few of the students felt comfortable speaking in English.

Then it was my turn. I gathered my collection, which made my hands dirty, and I proceeded to the front of the room. At first, the words got stuck in my throat, but the teacher kindly told me to take a deep breath and to just talk naturally. I think she forgot that talking naturally meant for me to talk in Greek, so I started, without thinking, talking in Greek. Of course she politely reminded me to use English.

This is what I told my schoolmates that day:

"My father and mother came from Greece. My father fixed things and had a respectable job in the vineyard. My mother was the daughter of the vineyard's owner. After they got married and had me, they came to America. There was a war in Greece and they just wanted to get out. The vineyard owner paid for them to come to America.

"When they arrived here, father did not have much. He began picking up things that were lying around. Some people thought he was a beggar and laughed at him, but he knew what he was doing. As he gathered things that people threw away, he started going to homes and barns to offer to fix their broken things. He made money, real money, and was able to move us to Colorado. My father taught me the value of saving even the smallest thing found on the ground.

"Even though my things here look like nothing important, someday I will use them to fix things like my father and make money. Father says that no matter where we go or where we live, there are always things to fix. I will be a handyman, just like my father. Even though he works in the mine, he is always asked to repair things, and the mine owner sometimes pays him in real money. Father says that collecting pays off He says that nothing is too small to use someplace. I want to be just like him."

Then the questions began, and I was scared. One boy asked, "How do you know what to collect?" I said, "Anything you see on the ground." Another boy asked, "Where do you put all your junk?" I did not know how to answer the question because I didn't think of my collection as junk.

To me, nothing is junk. Everything I have is or will be useful. I tried to answer but the words got lost in my throat again. I could feel myself melting into a pile of liquid goo. The teacher saw my distress and said, "I think what he was asking is, where do you keep your collections?"

Stories from the Arroyos

I then stood straight and tall. I cleared my throat and said, "I have boxes and piles in my room. I have some things in father's work shed and in a dugout behind the house." I then went to my chair and carefully put my treasures on my desk. I don't recall hearing anymore students tell about their collections for the rest of the morning.

At recess time, a group gathered around me and began to ask me if I could fix some things for them. One person said that her mother had a broken butter churn and her father didn't have time to fix it. Another girl asked if I could replace a belt on a sewing machine. A small boy wanted to know if I could repair a wheel on his wagon. To all of them, I said, "I think I can. I will do my best to help you." I made a lot of friends that day!

So began my days as a young repairman. I will never forget that day—not the embarrassing part, but the part about the students gathering around me at recess and asking for my help. I felt important and respected.

CARNATION MILK

My name is Izaak and I am from Poland. I am eleven years old. In my family there are eight children. I see many Polish people who work here and they are hard workers. It is scary to go so far underground to get the coal. My older brothers and papa come home late each night with black faces. They are very, very tired. They do not complain, but they are not happy like they were in Poland.

In Poland, we had a small farm with grass and wheat, cows, chickens, horses, pigs, and dogs. We had a garden too. We grew all our food and had enough to share with our neighbors. We do not have any of these things here in America. We were poor in Poland but we were happy, until the soldiers came into our county and told us what we could and could not do. Papa thought that living America would be better for us. At least there we could free.

Some things in America are strange to me. The land is very dry. The sun is very hot. Colorado has pretty mountains that are bigger than the Alps in Europe, but Papa is always working and we never go to the mountains. It is strange to have pretty mountains to climb but instead Papa goes deep underground. In Poland, we danced and sang all the time, but here no one seems as happy. Papa says they have a lot on their minds, mostly how to feed their families and find a good house to live in and have the children go to school. Everything costs

Stories from the Arroyos

money, and no one has any. That is strange to me. How can you work and not have any money?

Papa sold our land and animals to bring us here, believing life would be better. Now we go to the store to buy milk. They must have strange cows in America. The milk comes in small cans with red and white markings on the outside instead of large milking pails. Why would anyone put milk in small cans and put it on the shelf in a store? Doesn't the milk go bad? I suppose it must not be bad because every family buys their milk this way. How can it be any good?

On the cans of milk there is a flower. I asked my friends what kind of flower it is, and they told me that it was a carnation. Then I figured it out. The milk in the cans comes from the carnation. I felt proud that I solved the mystery!

One day I asked my *matka*, or mother, as they say in English, about the flower. "What kind of flower is a carnation?" I asked.

"It is a pretty flower," she told me.

I thought about that for a while, and then I asked her, "Do carnations give milk?" She laughed and said, "No, a carnation is a flower. Flowers don't give milk."

Now I was puzzled. "Why does it say Carnation Milk on the can of milk?" Matka laughed. She said that it is just a picture that looks pretty so people will buy it. "But why," I asked again, "does milk come in a can?"

Matka smiled and said, "Because it is so hot here, the milk will spoil faster than if it is not in the little cans. She said it is called canned milk. Well then, I decided, the milk we had from cows must be called pail milk. This all still seems strange to me.

After we empty the cans and use the milk, we throw the cans in a barrel. When the barrel is full, a man hauls it to what they call a dump site. What happens to the cans then? They just get rusty. I think it would be better just to get a cow and skip the canned part.

I have so much to learn about being in America. Words are different. People are different. I am glad I am not different—or maybe to them I am different too. I have so much to learn. I like living here in America but I miss my country. Poland is a large country that is covered with trees and acres of farmland. It's so different here. It's extremely dry. Teacher says this is a desert.

Even though I like it here, maybe someday when I am older, I will go back to my homeland. I only remember the nice things about Poland. Matka remembers only the bad things. I think things can change, just like milk from cows and milk from cans.

COOKING AND BAKING

I am the youngest in my family. I have five sisters who tell me what to do, how to behave, and how to comb my hair. I am the only boy.

We get along swell except that I wish I had a brother. Everything in the house is so girlie and pretty that sometimes I leave my boy stuff lying around just to make the house feel like mine too. This always drives the girls crazy!

The good part about having sisters is that I don't have to do house cleaning. My papa always takes me along to visit his friends and do things like make repairs, dig holes, wire buildings for the mine, and all kinds of man things. I like doing all this with him, but as I have gotten older, I am finding out my interests are different.

My favorite thing to do is be in the kitchen, watching and helping with the cooking. Now that I am almost eleven years old, my sisters are showing me how to cook and bake. I can even put up fruit in Mason jars!

Once in a while, someone outside the family will tease me about my liking to cook, but I have never gotten into a fight over it. Sometimes the boys at school make jokes about it. When I bring fresh-baked cookies to school to share, everyone is grateful that I have a fondness for cooking and baking! There are lots of boy things that I like to do, like racing, baseball, hiking, and games, but if I had only one choice in the world of what to do, I would be cooking and baking!

One day, two of my sisters and I wanted to surprise mother with a birthday cake. Of course, it wasn't her birthday. We just wanted to bake something so we used that as an excuse.

We got the flour, baking soda, baking powder, salt, nuts, cinnamon,

pumpkin, nutmeg, sugar, buttermilk, eggs, and a large bowl. We began to mix everything just like we once watched mother do. Mother never measured anything because, as she said, "After cooking and baking for so long, you just know how much of everything to put into it."

So we did as she did. We put in a pinch of this, a cup of that, a sprinkle of something else, and a dash of a few other things. It sure smelled good! Our batter was ready to be mixed. The girls said that I could do the mixing. After I grabbed the bowl of gooey stuff and started pushing it through my fingers, one of them asked me, "Did you wash your hands before you started?" We all learned in school about washing hands.

I said to her, "Of course I did. I washed up this morning." She wrinkled her nose when I said that.

The batter took a long time to mix. My fingers were sticky and glued together. There was flour all over the table and all over me. My sisters just chattered the whole time, about people, school, boys, hair, and clothes while I did all the work. I didn't mind though because I was the one who was having all the fun.

After the batter was mixed and the table was a mess, I poured it into a round pan. I had too much batter in the bowl and it ran over the sides. Someone grabbed another pan and I filled that one too. I still had batter in my bowl! My oldest sister said, "Let's just eat what's left in the bowl. Mother always lets us lick the bowl." So this is what we all did, only there was so much left in the bowl that we started to feel a little sick.

When the mixing bowl was finally empty, we put the pans in the oven. No one knew how to heat the oven, so we just guessed. No one knew how long to leave it in, so we just guessed again.

My sisters cleaned up the mess while I cleaned up myself. I had flour and sticky goop in my hair, on my shoes, all over my knickers, and, well, you get the idea.

There were some friends at the door, and I went to play with them. Someone yelled, "What about the cake?" I yelled, "I'll be back in a few minutes!"

My friends and I walked through the mining camp, looking for treasures that we can swap with our friends at school. We picked up bolts, pieces of paper with writing, dirty torn clothes, but found nothing we actually wanted to keep. Then I remembered the cake in the oven and rushed home!

When I arrived home, I found my sisters were gone and there was smoke coming from the oven. I panicked! I opened the oven door and burned my hand. *I am in trouble now!* I found a towel to pull the pans out and burned my other hand. I then realized the towels were a little wet. In my mind I could just hear mother saying, "Don't use a wet towel near heat; it doesn't protect your hand!" So with a burn on each hand, I put my hands in a bucket of water to cool them. The kitchen was filling with smoke and my cake pans smelled burnt.

One of my sisters came in the front door and screamed, "What are you doing? You'll burn the house down!" Then our neighbor to the west of us came in the house and screamed too. This was not helping the situation.

The neighbor grabbed a potholder and pulled the pans out, dropping one onto the floor. The cake was as black as a lump of coal! The pan fell onto the floor and the charred cake cracked the pan. *Now we are in trouble! Mother will be mad!*

When I was younger, I thought everyone ate the same as we did, but that is definitely not true. When I visit my friends' houses, I watch other mothers cooking and baking. I am learning about recipes from many countries, regions, and nationalities. I find this very interesting. I write down as much as I can, but my spelling is not the best. For the things I can't spell, I sometimes draw pictures. It works for me.

I have discovered that just about every nationality has a bread of some kind. Bread can be made from flour and corn (like tortillas) and rice (like rice cakes). Some breads use yeast and some do not. I don't know how this works, but I'll keep asking until I find out!

There are dozens of ways to prepare beef, pork, chicken, goat, and rabbit. There are dozens of ways to make vegetables. The only limit there is to what one can make is to make sure the food is available. Not everyone has a goat or a wild animal in their yard. Some vegetables are in season only part of the year. That is why people put certain foods in jars, so they can eat it all year round.

Right now my cooking is through trial and error. Everyone who cooks and bakes tells me that's how they learned too. So I am not discouraged.

I will continue learning about cooking and baking. Someday I plan to prepare an entire meal for my family. I promise it will be good! I probably will even try making another cake.

My dream is to be a cook in a big fancy restaurant in some big city. My goal is to have fun at what I do, not just to make money to live. I will make people happy by making their taste buds dance with joy!

Now, about that birthday cake. I think mother will have to decide which part of this whole birthday cake thing to get angry at first: the mess, the smoke, the waste, or the smell!

THE MINE DISASTER

My name is Annalina and I come from Sweden. For as long as I can remember, my father, brothers, uncles, and grandfather—in fact, all the men in our family—were always coal miners. I am not sure why we left Sweden. Moder and Fader, that is my mother and father as it is said in our Swedish language, have always liked adventure. I guess that is why we came to America.

Sweden is a truly beautiful country with a lot of hills and grassy fields. I was very young, about five years old, when we came here. I don't remember too much about Sweden. I have learned a lot more about Sweden since I have been in school in America. In school I learned that people left Sweden because there were too many people and not enough food. The people were poor, so I guess that is why we came here.

The area in southern Colorado is exceedingly dry this year and there are no green fields. It is always so hot and windy here. I like the winter months when it gets cold and we have snow. At least it is not hot then! I just don't understand why we left a beautiful green country for this dry desert land. Moder and Fader work so hard, I guess they don't even notice the difference. They never complain, at least not in front of us.

My Fader had been a miner forever. He was always careful and worked hard. The mine boss liked him and liked the whole family. Sometimes when he visited us at home, he was kind and courteous. He and fader talked a lot about mining. The boss appreciated my fader's ideas about improving the mining operation. Fader talked with him about the dangers of the coal dust exploding. They talked about using black powder for breaking up the coal in the coal seams. They talked about danger and safety. They even argued, but they never got mad at each other. Fader said this was because they were both "reasonable men."

One of the biggest fears for any miner who went underground was not coming out. Many things would go wrong in the mine shafts. Explosions from gasses created by the coal dust, rocks falling and trapping or crushing a miner, flooding, and cave-ins that block the exit were just some of the worries everyone had every day. Not only did the miners fear for their lives, but the families carried this fear with them as well. Moder said that some families have a plan in case an accident occurs. Other families just prayed that nothing would happen. I think this was good, but I think they needed a back-up plan in case the praying didn't work.

One day two years ago, the worst thing in the world happened. The mine had an explosion and a massive fire broke out. It was scary for everyone in the mine and in the camp.

I remember that day. We all heard the explosion and went running outside. People were running toward the mine shaft, carrying water buckets, and some men were getting the mule carts loaded with water barrels on them. Everyone was yelling and screaming and running. The air was thick with dust from the rocks. A strong wind whipped the smoke all around the area. It was hard to see exactly what was happening because it was all about a quarter of a mile away. It felt like it was much closer.

The miners who came out were injured and bleeding. They were coughing and choking. Some were burned badly. Many miners never came out. Fader was one of them.

The following days and weeks, there were many funerals. Some were only memorial services because some bodies could not be found in all the rubbish. Family members cried. There was a lot of sadness. Some families just fell apart. Some families were forced to move away. This was a very difficult time for everyone because we all lost friends, family members, neighbors, and school friends.

Even though we all knew the dangers, we always hoped this day would never come. Like all the other families, we survived the terrible loss of a family member. We had to go on living without having these people here with us.

It was a very sad time, and no one can know how all this feels unless you have lived through it. I am sure that in years to come, people will read about our mine disaster. They will only see it as an accident. They will read about the number of people who died. But they won't know how it felt or how hard it was to keep on going or the great sadness in our hearts.

Accidents in the mines were never the fault of the company. This was the company rule. It was always the worker's fault. In all the mine company reports, all the company ever said was "Explosion caused by miner's lamp" or "Miner fell into the path of runaway coal car" or "Miner crushed by falling rock." You never knew the truth, but for the company the truth was that every accident was the miner's fault. There was not any help to the family. No money, food, or benefits were given to help the family.

Usually when the miner dies or can no longer work at his job, the family must move out of the company house. We were lucky we did not have to move out of the camp. Moder said this was not luck but rather it was a blessing. The mine boss spoke to the company owner and found a job for Moder. He said she was a hard worker and that the school could use someone to keep the building clean. Moder was hired to be the janitor who cleaned the floors, dusted, and hauled the coal for the stove. The school never looked so good! We helped her with these duties. She never complained. She asked us to tell her if anything was not clean or proper, or if anyone complained about cleaning. She wanted it to be perfect. We were all so grateful that she had this job so we could stay in our home and did not have to quit school.

The mine boss visited us often to make sure we were doing all right. He would bring little presents for Moder like a sack of flour or canned goods. Sometimes he brought extra sewing material for her to make clothes for us. He was very kind to all of us. We liked him. Oh yes, he brought us candy and ice cream too!

Moder would use the food he brought to cook for him. As we ate the meal, he would tell us funny stories about mining. I never thought about mining being funny, but I guess if you look at situations in different ways, you can see good and bad, serious and funny in almost anything. I asked him about this. He told me, "I've learned that life is hard and I've seen so much suffering. It used to get me down. One day I met a man named Ray who helped me see that if I dwell on the sadness, I'll be a sad person. If I look at people and experiences as if they were part of something bigger, I'll be able to see a lighter or happier side of life. I thought this would put a sugar coating on the difficult times, but that is not what happened. I found that by looking at life in different ways, sometimes I help people not be so sad. I also learned from Ray that it doesn't hurt to change the facts a little so the stories are a bit more light-hearted."

The mine boss came to visit us often. Moder and the mine boss would sit at the kitchen table and talk for a long time. One time when they were sitting in the kitchen, talking, he said to her, "You are very beautiful. I like your blonde hair and blue eyes."

Moder laughed and replied, "That's because I am Swedish! We all have blonde hair and blue eyes." Then they both laughed. I liked to hear her laugh, and the mine boss always made her laugh. The mine boss was an honest man. I liked that about him.

As the years go by, the mining disaster is fading from my memory. I'll always love Fader and miss him. He taught me how to be honest and fair, say what I believe in, and not argue if I don't have to.

When I grow up, I will marry someone like my fader: a man who is kind, honest, and adventurous. But I will not marry a miner. Oh no, he can never be a miner! He will be a rancher or a businessman or a doctor, but not a miner. We will live far from the desert and wind. I wonder if there is such a place. Anyway, when I get married, my life will be different from what it is now.

GRANDMOTHER'S GIFT

In school, we learned about a famous man called Louis Pasteur. The teacher explained to us about how he discovered the cause of sickness. She said he had a microscope and looked into it. He found little tiny things moving around that he could not see without the microscope. He said these were bacteria, living creatures that can cause sickness.

Now my grandmother is a little old-fashioned, and she says this is nonsense. She says sickness is caused by lack of fresh air—that illness is from drinking too much, hanging out with saloon girls, not eating properly, not getting enough sleep, and staying out in the rain when you should have sense enough to come inside. I think she gets her information from her own experiences with people.

Grandmother uses her own medicine to make people well, just as she did in Mexico. She uses plant parts, leeches, mustard poultices, and oils. She also uses teas and powders, willow bark, and many roots. People call her a *curandera,* which means "healer" in Spanish. She is called this because her homemade remedies help people feel better and overcome sickness. Grandmother says this is a gift passed on from generation to generation and not everyone can be a curandera.

Once I watched her help a man who had a serious injury to his arm that was all red, swollen, and painful. She carefully washed it with something from a bottle and dried the wounded arm. Then she put wiggling leeches on it and covered it with a towel. Sometime later she removed the leeches and told the man to come tomorrow. This went on for several days. I was very surprised to see the wound was almost healed. I asked her how this had worked.

"The leeches eat up the poison that is in the wound," she told me. I asked, "Why didn't the man go to the doctor instead?"

She said, "He did not want the doctor to cut his arm off. The doctor would give him medicine, like morphine or aspirin, and maybe use a poultice of linseed oil to make it better. Most of the time the morphine makes a person sick, but it helps the pain. In the end, he very likely would have lost his arm."

All this makes me more interested in the sickness and healing process. Whenever I can, I ask people from different countries what they do when someone is sick or injured. Wow, am I ever learning a lot! I get to see how the treatments are done. I see how some sicknesses can be cured and that other sicknesses cannot. I am learning about healing plants, oils, and teas. The leeches are not my favorite as far healing is concerned, but I see how they are still useful.

When my puppy met a porcupine and got what seemed like a thousand quills in his face and neck, I learned how to pull these out. I learned what poultice (a type of homemade medicine) to put on him to bring the swelling down. He went from being a really sick puppy to being so full of life that he wears me out now.

Some of the things we don't have a cure for are small pox, diphtheria, typhoid fever, typhus, tuberculosis, and influenza. We don't even have a cure for a common cold! These diseases travel from one person to the next. No one knows for sure how this happens. When someone gets any of these, the house is quarantined, which means everyone stays home until the person is well. This is done so no one outside the family gets the illness. Sometimes entire families die.

Grandmother tells us the story about an epidemic in Europe called the Bubonic Plague. She says thousands and thousands of people died. This happened hundreds of years before she was born. Someone said it was caused by rats that had fleas, and the fleas bit the people. I think maybe that is why whenever someone sees a rat, he kills it right away.

Another story grandmother tells us is about the problem of cholera. This comes from drinking water that is dirty. Anyone can get this if he drinks from a river or lake, because in that water is bad bacteria from animal waste. People die because they get diarrhea and lose so much water from their bodies.

Grandmother says someday someone will find a cure for all these sicknesses. Then she says, "By then, my little Maria, we will all be in heaven because we will have died from something that years later could have been healed. We are just living at the wrong time."

When people have stomachaches, grandmother gives them ginger tea. Then she listens to them talk. I bet many people come to her just because they know she is a good listener. The tea probably helps a little too. She is a very kind and caring person. People love her.

When people are going to have a baby, they come to Grandmother. They ask her advice on how to have a healthy baby. Grandmother says many babies die when they are born or shortly afterward. Very often, the mother dies, usually because of too much bleeding. This makes me terribly sad because then there is no one to raise the other children in the family. In my Mexican culture, we all help take care of one another. It doesn't matter if ten cousins live in the house; no one is left out. We have a strong cultural belief that we take care of our people.

I want to do more than just help to heal injuries and make people well too. I want to show them that I care. I want their hearts to feel that I care. Grandmother does this by the way she talks and listens to people. She listens with her heart, and she smiles with her heart. I ask her how she does this.

"Well, first you listen," she started out. 'That means you must be quiet. You listen with your ears and with your heart. That means you must care about what they are telling you. You don't rush them, and almost always they tell you problems, fears, anxieties. They tell you about their families and husbands. Many times they just need to talk and you don't have to say very much. You can tell them it's all right to cry if you happen to see tears coming from their eyes. You remind them that there are people who care and that they are not alone. It is good to offer tea and a tortilla or something because people seem to talk more when they are eating. There is no magic to all this. The gift comes when you find yourself saying something to them, and they suddenly smile and they say, 'That's it!' or they say 'I can do it!' I think it is *santo momento,* a holy moment, where God is using you to help this person."

I really don't quite understand the holy moment idea that she talks about, but I've seen it work. I think about all this a lot. I'll keep asking questions. I want to help people in the way Grandmother helps them.

I've never met a lady doctor. I wonder if girls can be doctors. Either way, I'll continue learning from Grandmother. Maybe someday I can help heal people, both with home medicine and doctor medicine. Grandmother is not a doctor but everyone respects her and comes to her for help. She is good at what she does. Making people well again is what I will do too.

I will be known as the doctor who heals the body and the spirit.

MY ASSIGNMENT

I am in the seventh grade. Today the teacher has given all of us a writing assignment. He told us, "You must use the encyclopedias to look up something you want to learn and then write an essay about it, using some of the information you found." He is doing this only because the school just got a new set of encyclopedias. While this set of books is fantastic, with all the information and pictures, I prefer just to look at the pictures. Now we are being forced to actually *use* them to do work!

What will I write about? I will have to come up with a topic by tomorrow! Everyone is talking about this assignment during recess. Some people are excited to get started writing because they already know what they want to write about. Some girls are writing about clothes, life in the cities, cooking, houses, or different countries they lived in. Some boys are writing about coal mining, how to make beer, fish, baseball, and jobs they would like to do someday. I still did not have an idea.

When I start home after school, I take the long route, through the arroyo and over to the river. As I am walking, I am thinking, *What will I write about?* My mind is blank. The teacher said to look around and find something and to write about something I see or just page through the encyclopedias and find something that interests me. As I am walking, I look around and see things I have always seen: dirt, trees, flowers, sky, clouds. My mind is at a dead end.

In the arroyo, I climb over fallen tree limbs and fall on my face. I only get scratched and dirty, which is nothing new for me. As I walk on, I keep thinking, *What do I see that I can write about?* The topic has to be chosen by tomorrow!

Then it hits me! Right there in the arroyo! The trees! I can write about the piñon and juniper trees that grow in this area. My only hope is that the encyclopedias have information in there that can help me write something at least somewhat intelligent.

The next morning, I am very embarrassed to stand up in class. I pause for a second, take a deep breath, and say, "I'm going to write about piñon and juniper trees." No one laughs as I had expected them to.

The teacher smiles, nods, and says, "Excellent choice!" Well, I feel elated. Now I'm ready to start my research!

After getting to the P volume, I find a lot of information on the piñon. I am excited at all this information, most of which I didn't know. I also use the T volume and find just as much information. I am copying information like crazy so that when I get home I can decide which information I will use in my assignment.

After working for several hours, writing, erasing, and rewriting, my assignment is done. I am actually proud of what

I have written. I will write it here for you to read.

Piñon and Juniper Trees

Piñon and juniper trees grow in southern Colorado. Actually, they grow in other places too. They are not tall like trees in the higher elevations. They grow in desert regions called the Sonoran Zone, the Plains Zone. They grow in the high desert regions and by the foothills. They grow in rocky dry soil where rain is scarce.

The *piñon tree usually grows no taller than thirty feet or so. It is scrubby and has very rough bark. The tree grows slowly because of the climate. A piñon that is eight inches thick can be hundreds of years old. The tree produces the piñon nut, which has a delicate nutty taste. When the tree falls down, the wood is excellent for burning because it burns slow and hot. It smells very nice too.*

The juniper tree is used for wood and making utensils. It also does not grow to be tall. It looks like a cedar tree that can be found throughout North America. The juniper has berries that can be used for making a gin drink, but it has to be specially processed for this to happen. The Native Americans used juniper berries for what we today call diabetes. In the seventeenth century, the berries were used for breathing problems, like today's asthma. When the oils from the fruit and tree parts are distilled, they can be used as an antiseptic for wounds, upset stomach, cramps, and spasms. It cleans the blood of toxins. The oil also helps skin problems.

The Piñon and Juniper trees have helped people for hundreds of years. Since there are so many in southern Colorado, we can count on being healthy people.

All the students had to go in front of the class and read their papers. They wrote good papers. I liked hearing about the different countries and what the cities are like. Finally it was my turn. I began to read my paper to the class. I could feel my face getting red and hot while I was reading. I read slowly so as not to make a mistake in saying any of the words.

When I finished, I looked up at the class, and everyone clapped. I felt very pleased with my work. The teacher asked me how I picked my topic. I said, "I fell over a dead tree in the arroyo." Everyone just laughed. Anyway, he gave me an A+ and I felt good all day.

As far as writing another essay paper, I would say I am not in a hurry to do it. On the other hand, those volumes of the encyclopedia were certainly a great help. They have so much good stuff in them. I hope I can learn it all before I graduate!

THE FAMILY SECRET

We have a secret in our family. Mother says that father drinks too much and that he is not the same man when he drinks. He says it is really not her concern. Mother says he can't hold a job. He says he is a hard worker and the other men like him. She says he embarrasses the family. He says they should toughen up. She says he has no self-respect. He answers with, "Well, it's my life!" So the argument goes, every day and every day. Then mother cries and father walks out of the house, until it is time to eat.

People who see him laugh when he falls down or starts to act silly. He will sing and begin to dance. He sometimes teases the bar ladies. The worst is when he throws up. Yuck! If he does this in the house, my job is to clean it up because I am the oldest girl.

The kids at school tease me and say hurtful things about my father. I am embarrassed. Sometimes I just stay away from them. I feel stuck. I can't make him change. I can't make him stop drinking. The whole family is affected by his problem.

One day father and I were out walking along an arroyo, looking for arrowheads. He talked about the dry, windy weather, about coal mining, and about having a better life someday. I was afraid to ask him about his problem (as mother calls it), but I took a deep breath and asked, "Father, why do you have to drink all the time? It makes mother upset and makes her cry." Then he stopped. He looked at me with awfully sad eyes.

After a few minutes, he said, "I really don't know. Whiskey really tastes terrible but I keep drinking it. The white lightning that the bootleggers sell tastes even worse. But I can't say no to it. Don't tell your mother this, but I

feel like I've let everyone down. I really want to stop drinking. I have trouble working. Some people won't even talk to me because I owe them money. The company store doesn't want to sell us anything because they say I am so far behind on my bill and can't make enough to pay to them. It's a good thing the company boss says he could give me credit and trusts that someday I will pay."

We walked farther up the side of the arroyo and started across the dry field. The air was so hot and the wind was blowing dust up but we kept walking. I was thinking about what he said, and for a long time he didn't say anything.

Then he started talking again. "I guess I'm a disappointment to everyone— my ma and pa when I was young. My teachers thought I would become a businessman. I let them down. When your mother and I got married, everything was good and we were happy. After a while, I lost my job because the mine caved in. It was weeks before I found another job in another camp. I was the office manager in that company, but they fired me for taking scrip from the till. I just wanted a little more so I could feed all you children.

"Then we had to move. I think we moved seven or eight times just since you were born. I feel awful about that. I can't keep a job or support my family like a man ought to. I bet your mother thinks I am worthless. Yet she keeps me around. I'm lucky that way. She's a good wife."

Again we walked in silence. I was thinking about what he told me and began to feel sorry for him. In school we learned about having something called pride-for ourselves, our family, our work, and our country. I don't think father has any pride in himself. He's let people down and he drinks to forget.

I told him about what we learned in school about good pride, but I don't think he was listening. He didn't say a word all the way home.

The days passed and nothing was different

When I got home, Mother and Father were sitting at the table. They were unusually quiet. They both had been crying. I put my books down in my room. I then tiptoed back outside.

What could have happened? Did Father lose his job again? Did the company store demand their full payment? Did something happen in the mine? Was Mother expecting another baby? Did someone die? Did we have to move again? So many questions were running through my mind.

Later I went back inside, just before the sun began to set, because I was getting frightfully hungry. Momma hadn't even started making supper. Momma was gone from the kitchen. Where did she go? My mind began to fill with questions. I was working myself into a panic! *Did she leave us? Will my father raise me? Will I have to live with relatives back east in New York? Will I be sent back to Russia?*

Finally after what seemed like forever, I made a sandwich for supper. Father went to his room without eating. I could not find Momma anywhere. I called to Father, "Where is Momma? Is she coming back?"

He said from his room, "She is visiting some friends. She'll be back in the morning. We had a little argument. She left because she was angry with me."

Before I left for school the next morning, Momma came in the front door. She had been crying. Her face and eyes were red and puffy. It almost made me cry just seeing her like that.

Momma told me to sit down at the table. I slowly and quietly pulled out a chair. I didn't ask any questions. She called Father to come into the kitchen. He came into the kitchen and sat down. He did not make eye contact with either Mother or me.

Then the yelling started again. Suddenly it stopped. Momma spoke first. She said, "Father, I will not stay here if you keep on drinking. Our lives are falling apart, people laugh at us, you can't keep a job, and our child gets teased because of your drinking . . ."

As she stopped to take a breath, Father spoke up. "Okay, I'll try not to drink anymore. It's hard. It's very hard. I heard the other day that two other miners are trying to give up drinking. Maybe I could spend some time with them and we can help one another. It's hard giving up something you're used to, even if you don't like it. It's a bad habit, I know."

So this is what the situation was. Momma would leave us if Father didn't stop drinking. It seemed simple to me.

I walked over to his chair and put my arms around him. I whispered in his ear, "Please, Father. I'll help you if I can. Maybe we can take more walks, just you and me. Maybe all of us could go on more picnics and do things together, just the three of us. Please, Father, I love you, and I don't want to live in New York!"

Father looked at me with a puzzled look. "Why would you live in New York?"

My voice began shaking and I answered, "If you and Momma don't live together, I'll need a place to live, and the only other relatives we have are in New York."

Father hugged me and said, "You are not going anywhere. We're a family. I'll try to be a better father and husband. I'll need your help though." Momma and I both hugged and kissed Father, promising we would help him!

The next morning as I was leaving for school, I saw a broken jug not far from the house. I wondered if some town drunk smashed it to pieces. I found out later that Father had cleaned out his stash of jugs, and he and mother smashed the jugs against the rocks. I found out they had a good time doing it too.

THE WAILING WALL

My family is Jewish. My name is Esther. My father gave me this name because I was born on the fourteenth day of the twelfth month, Adar. In the Torah, Esther was a Jew who talked the king into not killing her people. She was a strong lady. Whenever we read from the Book of Esther, I am always proud to have her name. According to the story, she turned a day of defeat into a day of joy by helping to win against their enemies. This is also the Feast of Purim. We celebrate many days connected to important events in our Jewish history.

We have special times for family prayer and observe the Sabbath by not working from sundown on Friday until sundown on Saturday. We did this in the old country too. Father says it is God's command to His people. This is what we must do.

When we pray, Papa speaks and sings in Hebrew, which is the language of the Jewish people. We are called the Chosen People because God led Moses out of the desert and saved our people. I love all the stories, the prayers, and the singing.

Papa, his name is Mordecai, said the Jewish people have a wall in which they put pieces of paper, and then they stand and pray, asking for whatever they put on the paper. My people call the wall the Western Wall or *Kotel Ha Maaravi*. Other people call it the Wailing Wall. It is part of the wall that was around the old temple.

My people consider the wall to be one of the holiest places on earth. The Jews consider this place to be the most sacred of places, because the temple itself was thought to be the place where God resides on earth. Praying at the Wailing Wall is like being in the presence of the Divine.

Well, I have a wall that I go to every time I need to talk to God! I found it one day while walking in the arroyo. It is down the hill from my house. It can be reached only if you don't mind walking through brush and thorny bushes. It is part of an arroyo that takes a sharp turn before it goes down into the river. I walk every day, go down the hill, and find the wall. I put my piece of paper in the wall. Then I stand there awhile, talking to God.

I ask God to help my family. I ask him that we stay healthy, because there is only one doctor in the camp and getting sick costs money. I pray for Papa, that he doesn't lose his job again or get hurt in the mine, and we have to move to another camp. I pray for people to be nice and to help one another. That's about all I can pray for because I don't know how to spell too many other words. I suppose I could just talk to God without putting all my prayers on paper. Anyway, I like going to my own wailing wall. It is quiet and no one is around.

When I go to school, some people make fun of me. I don't understand why they do this. I am no different from them. When I play at recess, I usually find my Jewish friends and we play together. We understand each other. We don't tease one another like some of the other children do.

One difference I do see between my family and others who do not believe as we do is that they eat different food. We don't eat pork or shellfish. The meat and dairy products may not be combined. The meat must be ritually killed—that means in a certain way by certain people—and then salted to remove all traces of blood. We have a butcher in the camp that prepares all of this meat for us. Also, our food must be Kosher. I am not sure what that means. When I find out I will let you know. I only know that sometimes Mother and Papa argue about some things Mother buys at the company store. She tells him, "But we have to eat something when the butcher doesn't have our food."

We worship in our homes because there is no synagogue in this area. The closest one is in Trinidad.

We keep to ourselves. We do not tell others what to believe. We are not a secret group but we don't go around trying to get other people to join us.

People just don't understand us. I think it might have something to do with history. Hate for the Jewish people goes way back in history.

Father says that someday maybe I will travel to Israel and the holy places of our people. I am looking forward to that day!

LA FAMILIA

I will try to tell this story in English just like I am learning in school. Forgive me if I use a Spanish word now and then because that is what we speak at home. *La familia* means "my family," and that is who I would like to tell you about because family is the most important part of my Spanish culture.

In the coal camp, there are many other families who have also come from the territories in Mexico. We traveled by trains and wagons to come to America. Some people even walked. We came because there was no work in Mexico, and *mi padre,* I mean my father, could not support our family there. We were very poor, like all the others who lived where we did.

Mi padre said that in the United States people lived in real houses, and they had furniture to sit on. Mi padre said we left our country to find a better life for the family. So many bad things were happening in our country. He said if we wanted to remain together, we had to leave Mexico.

There were many problems in Mexico. We lived in the country and we were farmers, but the rain didn't come. We lost everything. Food was scarce. We went days with only tortillas and water. Families shared whatever they had, but soon everything was gone. Many people drifted into the cities to look for work. The cities became crowded. Soon there were no jobs. Many jobs were only for the women because they could cook and clean for the rich people. Mi padre did not want this to happen to *mi madre*, my mother. He said he had pride. He would earn money to take care of the family.

Also in our country there were problems with cocaine, which was used as a pain medication. Some people started taking it to other countries and using it for other things instead of medicine. Fighting and killing over a medicine did not make sense to me, but then I am only twelve years old and I have so much to learn. Mi padre said that some of these people came to farms and raided them for food and *pesos*, I mean money, and they killed the farmers' families. Mi padre was afraid for our lives.

Mi padre said that the government took the farmland and claimed it as its own. It sounds like stealing to me, but mi padre said the government had so much power that it could do anything it wanted. "The rich got richer and the poor got poorer," he told us, "and now we have nothing."

He said there was political unrest. I was not sure what that meant. My little brother wanted to know if the political people had trouble finding places to sleep and that is why they are having "unrest." Mi padre laughed and said, "Unrest means the people are not happy or free and they want to fight back to save their families."

He told us that poor people did not go to school and learned only from their families. He can read and write only a little Spanish but no English. He speaks very little English, but we teach him the new words we learn in school.

Mi madre teaches all the girls to weave baskets, sew colorful Mexican clothes, and cook Mexican food. Mi padre teaches all the boys woodworking skills, working with metals, and farming. His time is limited because he works long days in the mines.

We are a large family, as are most Mexican families. When we get together with other families, we sing and dance and eat. My favorite is the eating. You never in your life ever saw so much food! We have tortillas, enchiladas, green chili, red chili, and tamales. The hotter the chili, the more we like it! Everyone likes the hot peppers, which we just pop in our mouths and eat whole. Our mouths get very hot and our eyes water. We see who can eat the hottest pepper.

My favorite is the sopapilla with honey. My mouth just waters thinking about eating one. I only eat the peppers because I like to be part of the fun and teasing.

The older people drink margaritas, cerveza, and homemade wines. Those who like weaker drinks have café de olla or café con leche, which is coffee with flavors added into it. For the younger ones, there are chocolate and fruit drinks.

Everyone in la familia dances. At community gatherings, we all dance every dance. I will tell you some of these in English because you probably wouldn't be able to say them in Spanish. Some of our dances are the Mexican Hat Dance, the Dance of the Deer, the Mexican Agricultural Dance, and many folklore dances. The musicians play all day and into the night. We just have to keep giving them mas cerveza, more beer, and they are happy.

Now, I will tell you more about mi familia. We pray a lot. We pray before meals; we pray after meals. We have a little shrine, a special place, in our house with a crucifix, a picture of Our Lady of Guadalupe, candles, and flowers. Everyone who is from Mexico has a shrine in their *casas*, I mean houses. We go to church together. No one stays home. We put on our best clothes when we go. We all get baptized. Our favorite saint is Our Lady of Guadalupe. In Spanish we call her *Nuestra Señora de Guadalupe*. The story is told that she appeared to Juan Diego, a poor peasant farmer in Mexico, and that makes her special to our people.

Another thing about our culture is that we respect our elders, the older people. They share their stories and teach us many songs. We must always speak politely to them. We want to learn their wisdom. That is our custom.

We take care of them. They live with us until they die. We do not send them away or ignore them. They are part of us, part of our heritage, and well, they are familia. We stay together.

Grandmother has lots of wrinkles. She tells us, "Every one of these wrinkles is earned. I have worried and prayed. I have worked long hours in the hot sun. I have cried tears at losing my babies, and I thanked *mi Dios* when they lived.

My grandfather's hands are calloused, old, and wrinkled. He is a respected man. He tells us he has worked in the fields since he was six years old. He earned his living farming the dry land and working long hours in the fields. He tells us that some years no rain came and the crops failed. "We did not give up," he tells us. "We did not move to the city just to live in a shack, like many others did. They got diseases and died. We stayed and prayed, and we asked for rain. The next year was usually better. Sometimes we had to move into the higher lands for greener fields. We did what we had to do." Then he becomes quiet and sad because he had to leave all this behind. Now he is too old to work.

One more thing I want to tell you is about school. In Mexico we had *multigrados,* which means there were many grades in one building with only one teacher. Most children went to school only a year or two and then left to help on the family farms. Even in the villages, we learned a little English, but only as much as we could in just a few years. Mi padre never went to school. Mi madre went to school for four years.

At the camp we live in, everyone goes to school, even the adults. We learn arithmetic, reading and writing English, science, geography and all kinds of other good things. The older students learn skills that will help them when they get a job later on. In the camp school, we have more teachers and the classes are divided by grades when there are enough teachers. We sit at long tables with benches. Some grades have real desks for each person! We all get real pencils! The teachers are very patient with all of us but they don't allow any mischief. When I get into trouble, I get twice the punishment: one at school and a worse one at home when mi madre finds out!

Mi familia is very important to me. I want to keep the traditions of my country but also want to learn as much as I can about being in America. Mi padre has a good job. Mi madre is happy. We have a house and food. We aren't afraid of soldiers coming to kill us or drug robbers stealing from us. Life is good here, and we are all very happy.

NO PRIVACY

I am the middle child of eleven brothers and sisters. I am eleven years old. Mother makes sure we all have good food and clean clothes. She sees it as her duty to make sure that we all go to school, at least until grade six. Some of my friends think this is ridiculous because they can quit going to school whenever their papa says they should. They then must go to work. Their papa says they have learned enough and life can teach them whatever they need to know.

I am in grade five now and next year I get to help father earn money for the family. That sounds like fun but I like school. I can read and write and do arithmetic. But I do not want to stop learning new things. My teachers are very helpful. They say I am good at writing (as you can see by this story) and doing numbers in my head. I am trying to figure out a way I can help my family and still stay in school.

Fridays are fun days at school. This is what our teacher calls it. This means that we do things differently during the day. In the morning, we might help other students with arithmetic. Older students practice reading to younger students, and younger students practice reading to older students. Recess might be ten minutes longer, too.

One Friday, the teacher announced that we had to tell a story in front of the class. The story had to be about something that happened to us, how we felt at the time, and what we learned from what happened. We had to be ready to tell a story by Friday afternoon!

I thought hard about what I could say. So many things happen every day that I just couldn't decide which story to tell. I was getting worried that I wouldn't have a story ready! I thought of something sad, something funny,

something about exploring the arroyos, and something about family. That was it! I could tell a funny story about my family!

When it was my turn, I stood in front of the class with my hands folded like I was taught to do. I focused on a mark on the back wall and started talking. Here is the story that I told the class that Friday afternoon:

Let me tell you about what it is like living in a camp house with a big family. We all live in camp houses that are owned by the mining company. Our houses are constructed the same. The houses have four rooms: a kitchen, living room, and two bedrooms. We have a small kitchen where we eat, visit with friends, and just sit around the table and laugh. There are eleven of us brothers and sisters. We have lots of stories to tell. Each time we tell a story, it changes so of the happenings are not actually as they happened.

In our house we have two bedrooms. Mother and father and the three youngest children sleep in one room, and six of us sleep in the other room. Our house has a living room but ours is also a bedroom for friends who need a place to spend the night. We do our living in the kitchen. The rooms are very small, and mother often says, "Be careful not to step on your baby brother."

We *have one part of a bedroom that is very small. Some families use this for a pantry to store food. For us, this room is divided with a curtain. There is a pot in there that is white with a lid on it. Usually we go outside to the outhouse to do our business, but sometimes at night, and in the winter, we use the little pot. We take turns emptying it into the outhouse in the morning.*

There is a wash pan in the little room so we can wash our hands when we come in from outside. On Saturday, we each have to wash up in that little room. We use the same water for three or four of us then throw it out and put in clean water. We all use the same towels. This is life in the camp house.

One day we all ate some bad food from the camp store. Mother said she got it at a good price. After supper and into the night, we all started to get sick. Mother felt really bad. With eleven of us and mother and father all sick, we all needed to use the pot at the same time. Some of us boys were able to run outside, but the little ones could not make it outside so they used the little pot. This just was not working! The room was too small! The pot was too small! The house smelled terrible! Come morning, we all were feeling a little better, but we were all tired. The little pot sure came in handy!

If I were to tell you that the best part of living in a camp house is the kitchen, this would be the truth. We have no privacy in our bedrooms. We have no privacy in the little room. Well, if I tell you the whole truth, there just is no privacy in this camp house!

A DIFFICULT DECISION

One day in October, father came home from the mine. He said there was talk about a strike. I sat at the table with my family and I listened to him tell us what was going to happen.

He said, "If we can't get more pay and better working conditions, some of the men said they would tell the company that they wouldn't work the mine. If we strike, then we could no longer live in our house because the company owns it. I don't know where we would live. Right now we don't have any money except the company scrip to buy food. We wouldn't be able to buy food from the company store or any other store. The scrip that we have would be worthless. I'm worried about what we'll do."

For a long time, no one spoke. Everyone looked sad. Father looked scared. He felt bad that he would not be able to provide for his family. Momma's eyes looked like she was ready to cry. Mother said to me, "Frederick, go do your homework. Father and I need to talk." I went to my room. I couldn't hear what they were saying.

I began to think about what was happening in the family. We have a nice camp house. Momma has made the house look pretty with pictures and curtains. We have beds to sleep on in our own room. We have lived here for almost four years. Momma always fixed good meals and served the meals on the dishes she brought with us from Germany. If we have to move because of the strike, we wouldn't know where we could live.

My father works in the Black Hole, as the miners call it. This means he works underground and digs the coal from the rock. Every day he comes home coughing. He has black coal dust smeared on his face, hands, and clothes. Father goes to work even when he is sick and can hardly breathe.

The camp doctor said he has Black Lung and will never get better. The mine boss just wants the coal. The boss doesn't care how he gets it. If my father cannot work anymore, someone else will be hired in his place and father would be out of a job. This worries him all the time.

The company pays fifty-five cents for every ton of coal he brings out of the mine shaft. The is money doesn't go far. He told us that all the miners have to pay for their own tools, even the blasting powder. Sometimes they need to shore up a shaft with timbers. This means some days no one gets paid. Sometimes there are cave-ins and workers get hurt. Some men are even killed.

Father says that the only time he can stand up is when he goes into the mine shaft and when he comes out of the mine shaft. All day he is on his knees or on his back. But he never complains around us. He is a hard worker, and the company boss approves of the work father does.

As we sat listening to my father, I found myself getting mad at the company. I said, "They should be nicer to the workers."

Father only looked at me and said, "That is why we might go on strike. We need more money and safer working conditions. Too many people are injured and then fired. No one can break rock with only one arm or one leg."

Father looked at Momma and me and said, "I don't know where we will go. I just know that things will change in the camp. The company boss is getting very angry and upset with us. Someone said he is trying to break us. Who knows what he'll demand from us. Who knows what it will be like after this is all over."

Momma got up and started fixing some supper. "We might as well eat while we still have food," she said, almost choking as tears ran down her face.

No one talked much during supper. No one ate much either.

Father left for work the next day before the sun was up. He was very quiet. We all went about our usual chores, and then I went off to the camp school. Everyone was talking about the strike and most everyone was excited. I was not. Many of my school friends were talking about living with relatives in the big cities like Pueblo or Trinidad, some moving to Colorado Springs.

We didn't have relatives in the big cities. I didn't want to leave my home here.

That night father looked very discouraged. He said the strike would happen in one week if the demands were not met. He said he didn't want to be part of it. There might be violence, and workers and their families would get hurt.

We began to make plans. We would have to leave our house. I would have to leave my friends at school. Father said he could maybe get work in another mine that was farther south. He had a friend with a team and wagon that he could hire to move us. Father said, "We can only take what fits into the wagon and what the horses can pull."

As the days passed, Mother was busy putting clothes into wooden boxes. We did not have many clothes but she wanted the clothes to stay clean on the trip. She also put letters and important papers together in bundles tied with string.

The hardest to pack were the things in the kitchen. Mother had pans, pots, ladles and spoons, big knives, and eating utensils. She packed what she could. These were all boxed up and put by the front door.

The items that took her the longest to pack were the dishes she had from her old country. They were blue and white, decorated with pictures of the German countryside. Mother loved those dishes. Some had gotten chipped from so much use. Some had broken handles but were still useable. As she took each dish off the shelf, she looked it over, turning it in every direction, examining it to see if she would take it along.

At the end of the day, mother finished the packing. She decided to leave some of the special dishes in the house, hoping maybe the new owners could use them. Mother is like that—always thinking of someone else, no matter how hard things were. She has the biggest heart in the world.

Father cleaned the junk in the yard and put it in a pile, which we would haul to the dump behind the stables. He packed his tools, leaving nothing behind.

On Saturday the wagon came. Everything was loaded into it. Father said that mother had done a good job packing the boxes.

It was hard saying good-bye to our neighbors and friends. We all cried, except father. I think he was trying to be strong. He has a big heart.

As we drove away, some men were yelling, "Don't go. We need you for the strike!" Other men were yelling things that I did not understand, saying my father was giving up and running away from a fight. All I know is, father was trying to take care of his family. That's why we were leaving.

When we were away from the camp, I could see tears in my father's eyes. No one talked after that. The only noise you could hear was the tin clanging, wooden boxes bumping together, the leather on the horses' harnesses rubbing, and the spring on the squeaky bench we were sitting on.

It was a very sad day for us.

THE HAUNTED HOUSE

The camp I live in is just for us Negroes. Do not ever call us anything else. I've seen so many fights and people dying over words that we have been called that it really makes me mad.

We live in a mining camp that is set apart from the other camps. We like that because then we can be ourselves and not what others want us to be.

We have our own kind of food. We like deep fried chicken and dumplings with lots of vegetables. We eat pigs feet, barbeque, smothered pork chops, bell peppers, and beef stew. We each have a small garden near our house. They are fenced in because of the roaming chickens and stray animals.

We have our own way of worshipping. We sing a lot and say "Amen" and "Hallelujah" through the service. We clap our hands and sway. Some people even faint they get so excited. The longest part is when the preacher talks and tells us about being sinners and needing to repent. Sometimes he really works himself into a lather because he talks so much. He tells us to be good and to tolerate those not of our kind. Most people I know are kind, so I'm not sure what he means.

The best part of living here is all the grown-up stories. My favorite is about when my aunt lived in the South and was a slave.

She said the master's house was haunted. She had to live in the house and work there until she was set free or died, whichever came first. Mamie was only thirteen years old at the time.

My Aunt Mamie tells the story like this. She lived in the servants' section of a house, a short distance from the main house. The main house was huge.

There were more rooms than anyone ever needed. The servants' job was to keep these rooms clean. Every day, the servants had to scrub floors that weren't even dirty. They had to polish silver. The rich owners always had a lot of silver to polish.

One of Mamie's jobs was to go to the garden each morning to pick the ripe vegetables for the day's meals. Mamie always found nice ripe vegetables. She put them in her pail and carried them to the kitchen. Whenever she walked through the back door (which was for the servants and other colored workers only), her pail would get extremely heavy, as if someone had put rocks in it. Mamie would grab on with both hands and manage to get it to the kitchen. The cook took the fresh vegetables. She always gave Mamie a cookie for her help. Mamie would help the cook peel and cut the vegetables and listen to her sing and tell stories.

The same thing happened every day when Mamie walked through the back door. This scared her so much that she told the cook what happened when she came in through the back door. The cook looked at Mamie and said, "Child, it is just a ghost of some master still trying to make things hard for our people. Don't let it win. You keep your head up and keep going right through the back door. After a while, the ghost will know it can't stop you, and it'll find someone else to bother."

Now this story might not scare you, but it makes me glad I don't work for a master. This reminds me that ghosts can bother you any time, no matter who you are. Everyone has stories about ghosts and haunting. I hear so many stories and only believe half of them. I keep going to church and praying that they don't come after me!

I hear tell that the camp down the road has a haunted house too. It's the boss's house. Every time a worker is called into that house, no one sees him again. Rumors say people are buried under the house. Other people say the men are just fired and sent out of the camp. Believe whatever you want, just don't go in that boss's house!

A SAD STORY

My twin sisters were born in January. Now I have seven sisters. My name is Gabriel. I am the oldest. Mother said I need to take care of my sisters until she is able. The camp doctor said she must rest in bed for a week since the birth was so hard on her.

I am eleven years old. I can cook and clean the house. I help with the laundry. Someday I will have a big family of my own, and I will know how to take care of my family. Right now I am still learning all the things I need to know. Mother says I am a fast learner. The only thing I have learned all the way is how to can pickles, tomatoes, and apples.

My Aunt Isabella came from New Jersey to help us while mother was in bed recovering from the twins' birth. She knows all about babies because she is a nurse in a hospital in New Jersey. She even helps deliver babies! While she is here, she tells us stories. I can never hear enough of her stories. Someday I will go to New Jersey and see everything she is talking about.

Before mother was able to be out of bed, we prepared to have the twins baptized in the church. The baptism brings them into the Church and makes the family raise the children in the faith. I was baptized right after I was born too.

A neighbor offered to make baptismal dresses. The dresses were long, very white, and very pretty. Mother held the dresses in front of her and had tears in her eyes. She said, "They are the most beautiful dresses I have seen since coming to America! Thank you for all the careful hand-sewing. These must have taken you hours! I will pay you when I can."

The neighbor said, "No need to pay me. Remember, in Italy, friends always gave these as the baptism gift. I was honored to make the dresses."

The baptisms took place on Sunday. Mother didn't stay in bed the whole week. I'm glad she didn't because all the work was tiring for me. All week I kept thinking about how hard Mother works and no one ever says thank you. Ialso thought a lot about what kind of family I would have when I got married. The only thing I want is a big, happy family, just like the one I live in now.

The twins were dressed in their beautiful dresses. The baptism was a time when everyone was happy. The neighbors came over and brought food. We celebrated all day.

Mother was still weak but she took care of the twins while I did the cooking and cleaning. I had to stay home from school to help out. Father said he was proud of me for all the things I could do to help mother.

Mother saw a bad rash on her arms, then on her face. She started to feel hot and sick. After just a day, the rash had leaking pimples. Father called the camp doctor.. After examining Mother, he took my father into another room and said, "She might have chicken pox, but I think it is worse than that. She might have smallpox. Her symptoms are more like smallpox." Father remembered that one of the new neighbors at the celebration had a rash and he looked pale, but father did not talk to him very much that day. He was new to the camp. The doctor said he needed to see this man right away.

It was bad. Mother said smallpox is "catchy" and the whole family could not leave the house. Father was upset because he might lose his job if he didn't go to work. The doctor said he would talk to the camp boss and tell him the situation.

Most of us got the rash but the rash did not have pimples. That is, all of us except the twins. They were so small and they got the rash and pimples. The doctor, Mother, and Father all looked very serious and were extremely worried. Father looked scared; Mother was crying. Yes, the twins had smallpox. They died the following Saturday. The doctor said they never had a chance. They were too small and too young to fight it off.

Mother tried to be strong, but it was hard. She cried a lot. We all did. It was a very sad time, and I will never forget the sadness in my mother. I

loved my twin sisters. I will miss them even though I only knew them for a short time.

I dream of the day when there will be no more sickness or hardships that make people cry. Life is challenging enough without having all these extra difficult things.

THE SLINGSHOTS

I have only brothers so I tag along with them and do everything they do— only better! I brag a lot, but really I am good at lots of things. My name is Danica. I am eleven years old and I can outrun any boy my age. I can play baseball better than anyone my age. I can spit farther. I can ride a mule and a horse. I can jump farther across some arroyos. Just give me a challenge and I can outdo most anyone my age!

Mama told me that I should learn girl things and learn to be a lady. That's the way it was in the old country of Slovenia. Girls were girls and boys were boys. Everyone learned to do the things that were expected of them. They had to learn to act a certain way. This was just the way it was.

Well, we are in America now. I see that things are different. I learn in school about all the things a person can do, like to be a shopkeeper, a doctor, a boss, a rancher, a preacher, and so many more things. I want to learn to do so many things!

One summer, six of us decided to make slingshots. We found some piñon branches that were still strong. We cut them into Y-shaped pieces that we could hold in our hands. We looked through

Stories from the Arroyos

the dumps behind camp and found some rubber from an old bicycle tire. The tire had an inner tube that had a hole in it. It already had a dozen patches on it. The person who owned it just gave up on fixing it again.

We got a knife and cut strips out from the tube. The strips were about eight to twelve inches each, give or take an inch. We took our knives and cut one-

inch slits on each top part of the Y. We doubled the rubber through each one, kind of making a loop for a sling. We had some great slingshots.

We went back to the dump and picked up dozens of bottles, mostly from the saloon. Some were clear and some were green or brown. We each picked up a handful of small stones. We set the bottles up on a ledge near an arroyo and tried shooting stones at the bottles. It took a long time before anyone actually hit a bottle. We laughed and teased each other about how bad we were at shooting.

We gathered more small stones and practiced all afternoon. We actually managed to hit a lot of the bottles and smash them to pieces. What a mess of broken glass pieces we made!

Then we ran out of bottles. We went behind the company store and found some more bottles in a crate. That made it easier to carry. We carried three crates of bottles to our target practice place. We shot more stones. By this time, we were all pretty good at hitting the bottles.

When we ran out of bottles again, someone (not me!) started shooting stones at one of the boys. This started a fight and then it wasn't fun anymore. I went home.

At school on Monday, the teacher told us about a problem at the company store. Someone had stolen three crates of bottles belonging to the store. These were going to be returned to the supplier for a refund. By doing this, the company store could keep the cost down so families wouldn't have to pay so much. That day we had a lesson in reusing things and not wasting anything. I thought we did a fine job of reusing the bottles for practice.

No one said anything at recess. No one came can forward and told what we did. We were all feeling a bit guilty. There was talk in the camp about troublemakers. We never came forward.

On Saturday, we all decided to go over to the company store and offer to help the owner scrub the floor and dust the shelves. He was very happy to have the extra help in cleaning. We were happy that he let us work. Of course, we didn't take any payment for our work.

I think he might have guessed the reason we were so willing to help, but he never said anything. As for our slingshots, we still use them once in a while for a contest or something fun. Now we are more careful. Now we use bottles from the dump, and only from the dump.

THE MINE CLOSING

Everyone knew this day was coming. Eventually every mine runs out of coal. The owner of the company reported that there has been less and less coal taken out of the mine shafts. The bosses say the miners and their families can go to other mines and work.

My *vater* (father) and *bruder* (brother) have worked in this mine for five years. I listened to their stories. I decided that maybe it is good that the mine is closing because they have trouble breathing, and their skin and clothes never come clean from the coal dust. They don't laugh much anymore either. Coal mining is very hard. Don't let anyone tell you it is easy.

I am happy that they worked in the mine because some good came from it. We have a good house and room for everyone. We have good food from the company store. We have a community hall where we hear music and go dancing. I go to a good school. Mostly, I have good friends who I hope will move into the next camp with us when we find one.

I don't make friends easily; at least that is what the teacher said. She said I am a loner. Let me say this, I do make good friends when

I decide who will be my friend. Just because someone wants to be a friend doesn't mean that they will be good for you. I learned that the hard way in the last camp we lived in. A couple of students who wanted to be friends got me into trouble by having me steal from the company store. They said, "If you really want to be our friend, this will prove it." My vater always told me to be honest. I was confused. Why were they asking me to steal? Vater said to just tell them no and that I should go find other friends who want to do only good things that are honest. He said you should be helping people, not hurting them. At the time I was only seven. I did not understand, but I knew Vater was always right so I listened to him.

Vater says the mine owners only care about making money. That is why he gets so little pay. Vater can bring out sixty-six thousand pounds of coal in one day. After the company store gets its share of his pay, after the doctor gets his amount, after he pays for renting his tools, and after paying the house rent, Vater figured he made two cents a ton for his work. That's just not right to pay so little for all that hard work.

Even though I am only eleven years old, I am teaching my vater and bruder to read English. They can only read German now. We speak German at home, but outside of the house we try to speak English. Some people give us credit for trying to speak good English. Other people laugh at our strong German accents. They say we sound funny when we talk. Well, I think they sound funny, but I won't laugh at them!

I hope the next camp has good places for baseball and arroyos to explore. This camp is great for all that! I'd like a camp without wind, but as long as we are in this area of Colorado, the wind will always be here. Vater says to make friends with the wind. I wonder what he means.

I hope at the next camp, Vater will be paid in real money. Then he can try to put some away so we can leave the coal mines and move into the city. There is so much more to do there: better schools, more stores, and hundreds of people—at least that's what I am told. I could get new clothes once a year and maybe a new pair of shoes. Mine are so worn out that I put cardboard in the bottom. It really is

Stories from the Arroyos

bad when it rains and there is mud. My feet are wet all day! At school I can't think about lessons when my feet feel so awful. It just messes up my whole day!

Vater and Bruder are packing our belongings in canvas bags. Vater got some of these bags when he was in the war in Germany. He never talks much about the war except to say he is glad to be in America and not living in fear of what will happen next.

As we pack up, I start feeling sad because I will miss my home here. This is the only place I know. Mater (mother) died when I was born, and Vater and Bruder have raised me the best they could. Vater is proud of me. He wants me to stay in school and do more with my life. I will obey him because he is the boss of the family!

I hope we have electricity in the next camp. The oil and kerosene lamps that we use give off an awful bad smell. It makes our clothes and skin smell so bad that we don't like being inside. I hear that electricity can be turned on with a switch or the turn of a knob. I wonder how that works.

The most exciting part of the mine closing is watching the houses being moved. The houses are loaded onto platforms and moved into the nearby town. It takes a week or more to move one house. All that remains is the foundation.

I like watching and listening. The men who do this work use words I've never heard before. I tried to remember the words and use them at home. That was a bad idea because Vater said these words were not used by educated people. I used one of the words at school and the teacher's mouth fell open in shock that I would say such a thing. I didn't know it was a forbidden word to use in school. She said, "People who swear are not smart enough to think of a better word." I learned my lesson. When Vater found out, he punished me for using curse words in school. I decided to study harder in school so I could learn better words to use.

Vater says the mine closing is a blessing in disguise. He said working here was hard on his body. He is hoping he can find some other kind of work. It is springtime and he says he would like to work outside in the fresh air. Vater and Bruder both say they would work as ranch hands somewhere in the area. I will still go to school but I will have chores to do in the morning before I go. I am so excited about this that I can't wait to go.

I like a blessing in disguise. It opens up a new door and gives us a chance to try something different. Instead of being sad about not staying in the coal camp, I am excited about all the great possibilities ahead.

Reflection and Discussion for

STORIES FROM THE ARROYOS

BY KATHRYN CARPENTER

These reflection and discussion questions can be used in classroom discussion or simply shared among the readers who wish to find a deeper meaning in these stories.

1. Which story was your favorite? Why?
2. What would you say is the lesson you learned in your favorite story?
3. If you were the person in the story, describe what you feel like. How would you talk? What would you look like? How would you dress? How is this different from what you feel and look like today?
4. What do you think are lessons to be learned in the other stories?
5. Which character in these stories did you like the best? Which character did you not like? Can you explain why you think or feel this way?
6. Try using your imagination to create a different ending for one of these stories.

7. Make a list of as many differences as you can between how life was then and how it is now.
8. How would you feel about moving to another country? What things would you have to learn?

ABOUT THE AUTHOR

Children learn to love reading at a very early age. Parents and siblings read them stories at bedtime or just while relaxing in a chair. When books were scarce, storytelling filled this gap. Reading changes a person from being focused on immediate concerns to looking to the past and the future.

Kathryn Carpenter has been interested in reading since starting school back in the days before computers. Of special interest to her is historical fiction. Since moving to southern Colorado, she has immersed herself in trying to understand the people who lived in this coal-mining area.

She is presently a professor at Trinidad State Junior College, teaching in the nursing department. Her personal history includes teaching in elementary education, ministering in pastoral services, and serving in health care. She is a member of A New Genesis Community from Green Bay, WI. Combining these rich personal experiences enabled her to write these stories of historical fiction in the hopes that they bring the reader closer to experiencing life from the eyes of the children living in the coal camps in 1900.

www.ingramcontent.com/pod-product-compliance
Ingram Content Group UK Ltd.
Pitfield, Milton Keynes, MK11 3LW, UK
UKHW061622240426
12048UKWH00048B/1623